The Pope in Canada

The Pope in Canada

Introduction by the Most Reverend J.M. Hayes, J.C.D., D.D.
Archbishop of Halifax
Co-Treasurer,
Canadian Conference of Catholic Bishops

KEY PORTER BOOKS

Canadian Cataloguing in Publication Data

The Pope In Canada

ISBN 0919493-46-7

1. John Paul II, Pope, 1920–   -   Iconography.
2. Popes — Voyages and travels — Canada — Pictorial works.
BX1378.5.P66 1984   262′.13′0924   C84-099544-X

Key Porter Books
70 The Esplanade
Toronto, Ontario
Canada M5E 1R2

Design: Don Fernley
Typesetting: Imprint Typesetting
Printing and Binding: Sagdos S.p.A.
Printed and bound in Italy

84 85 86 87   6 5 4 3 2 1

Page 1: Pope John Paul II greets schoolchildren at Notre-Dame Basilica in Montreal.

Page 2: At the open-air mass at Quidi Vidi, near St. John's, Newfoundland.

Page 5: Pope John Paul II aboard the *Luigi Pirandello*, an Alitalia airliner, before arriving in Canada.

Page 6: Inside the Ste Anne de Beaupré Basilica.

Contents

Introduction

It is a pleasure to introduce a book which records the historic visit of Pope John Paul II to Canada.

Both the visual images and his message to Canadians reveal the love of His Holiness for Canada and its people. The young, the aged and the handicapped draw an immediate response. But none are excluded whether they profess his faith, another faith or none.

In every region of Canada and to every group, native peoples, legislators, diplomats, clergy, religious, laity, there is an unmistakable theme. It is that Jesus Christ is the Lord who reveals God to humanity and humans to themselves. In Him they discover their dignity and destiny. From Him, derive the ethical imperatives which can create just societies, respect for human rights and peace in the world.

It is my earnest wish that all who read this volume will draw from it this message of hope which is its heart.

Most Rev. J.M. Hayes, J.C.D., D.D
Archbishop of Halifax
Co-Treasurer
Canadian Conference of Catholic Bishops

Quebec City

The white-robed figure descended the steps from his airplane, kissed the ground at Ancienne-Lorette airport, and was greeted by a twenty-one-gun salute. So, on September 9, 1984, began Pope John Paul II's twelve-day tour of Canada, home of 11.4 million Roman Catholics.

The delegation that welcomed the Pope to Quebec City and Canada included Governor General Jeanne Sauvé; the Most Reverend Louis-Albert Vachon, Primate of Canada and Archbishop of Quebec; Prime Minister John Turner; Quebec Lieutenant-Governor Gilles Lamontagne, and Quebec Premier René Lévesque.

In her greeting, Jeanne Sauvé welcomed the Pope as a pilgrim of compassion and peace. The Pope replied that he came not as a head of state, but "above all, as pastor and brother."

Later that day at Laval University, Pope John Paul commented on the significance of Quebec City: "Here was the first diocese of North America. It is from here that the seed first sown began its immense growth." The date of the tour was also historically significant: in 1534 Jacques Cartier arrived in Quebec and planted a thirty-foot wooden cross. Four hundred fifty years later, Pope John Paul II arrived to offer "the light and strength of faith in Jesus Christ."

Prime Minister John Turner (*above*) and Governor General Jeanne Sauvé (*right*) were among those to greet the Pope at the airport, along with members of the Royal 22nd Regiment (*previous page*). In her welcome (*left*), Jeanne Sauvé called on Canadians to "join the unflagging ranks of those who pray and ... work for peace."

Also at the airport to greet the Pope were children attired in the dress of their cultural heritages. They presented him with flowers and gifts.

The first stop of the papal tour was Cartier-Brébeuf Park, the site of the first Jesuit residence in Quebec. There he met a group of newly confirmed young people (*above and overleaf*) who waved yellow cardboard doves bearing the names of other children who had been confirmed in Quebec parishes last spring. Accompanying the Pope on his tour through Quebec City was Louis-Albert Vachon, Primate of Canada and Archbishop of Quebec (*right*).

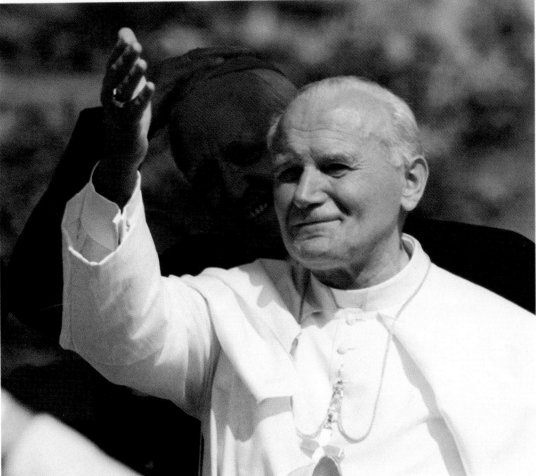

Crowds thronged the route through Quebec City as the Pope passed by in his specially constructed, Canadian-made vehicle, dubbed the "pope-mobile" by the press.

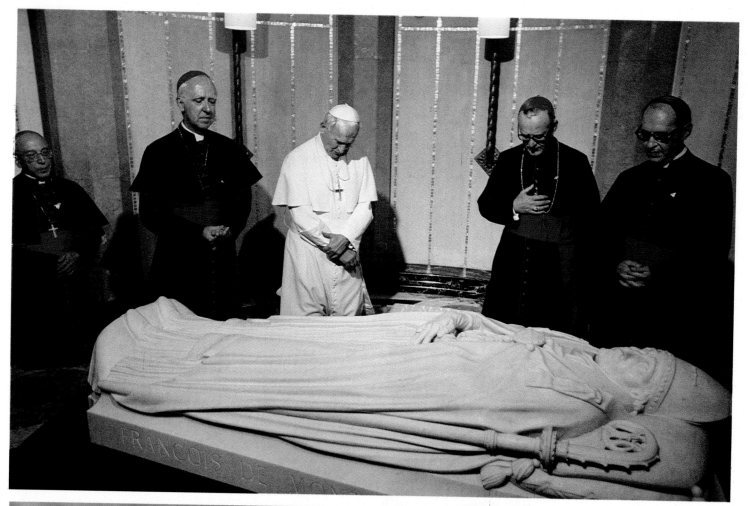

At Youville Square at the gates of the city wall, the Pontiff unveiled a plaque (*left*) dedicated to François de Laval, the first bishop of Quebec in the seventeenth century. Later, he visited Laval's tomb.

Two hundred fifty thousand attended an open-air mass at Laval University (*previous page*). As he climbed the red carpeted stairs (*left*), the Pope was accompanied by Archbishop Vachon. In his homily the Pope urged his audience not to divorce faith and culture. Faith, he said, plays a great part in culture, which is "the soul of a nation." The sun set as the mass ended (*right and overleaf*).

The second day of the papal tour began with a visit to the Musée du Québec (*above*). Accompanied by Archbishop Vachon and Premier René Lévesque along with Quebec bishops, the Pope toured the exhibition of sacred art.

At the François-Charon Centre (*right*), a rehabilitation centre for the handicapped, Pope John Paul stated: "The handicapped person is a human subject with all the innate, sacred and inviolable rights that that entails." He linked his call for handicapped rights to his opposition to abortion and mercy killing. Before the speech, he moved among those gathered, touching their hands and faces.

From Quebec City, the Pontiff traveled by limousine to the shrine of Ste Anne de Beaupré, where he met with Indian and Inuit representatives and received gifts from them.

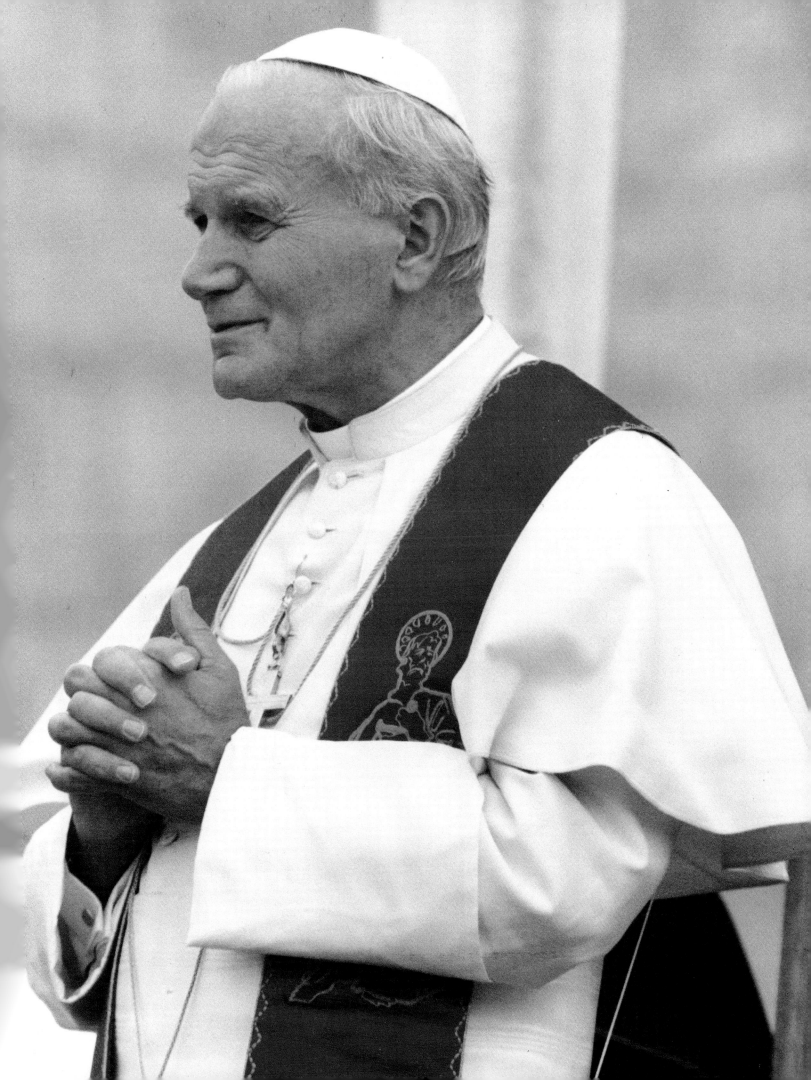

The Pontiff's message to the
Inuit and Indians gathered at
Ste Anne de Beaupré recog-
nized past difficulties and
"blunders" in the native peoples' encounters with the
Church, but called on them to
let the Gospel enrich the spiri-
tual qualities that are distinc-
tive to their cultures.

Trois Rivières

Tens of thousands of people stood in the cold rain at Cap-de-la-Madeleine, near Trois Rivières, to see the Pope in the late afternoon of September 10. The national shrine, considered the most important in North America, is devoted to the Virgin Mary. In his homily John Paul spoke of the importance of faith. At Notre-Dame-du-Cap, he expressed the hope that "the streams of the faithful who come here to pray never run dry." Each of his visits abroad, the Pope added, are marked by a similar pilgrimage to a great shrine to the Virgin. After recovering from his gunshot wounds in 1981, John Paul traveled to Fatima in Portugal to thank the Virgin Mary for his life. In Poland he sent his bloodied sash to a Marian shrine in Czestochowa.

After the mass, the Pope reboarded the train for Montreal.

The rain became a special part of the mass celebrated by the Pope at Cap-de-la-Madeleine near Trois Rivières. Asking the audience to ignore the weather, he told them that rain is the biblical symbol of grace. At Cap-de-la-Madeleine, the Pope paid homage to the Virgin Mary.

Montreal

Throughout the tour the Pope met many groups, young and old, men and women, clergy and laity. He rarely relaxed from a grueling pace that more befitted a young U.S. presidential candidate than a sixty-four-year-old pontiff. On the evening of his arrival in Montreal, he visited Mary Queen of the World Cathedral. The next morning at 8:15 he was at St. Joseph's Oratory, where he spoke to 3,500 priests and seminarians, then on to the Mother House of the Sisters of the Congregation of Notre Dame. At 10:30 he celebrated the eucharist at Jarry Park before 350,000. In the afternoon he was warmly and loudly greeted by school children at Notre-Dame Basilica, after which he met with 60,000 fifteen- to twenty-five-year-olds at Olympic Stadium.

Everywhere the response was enthusiastic and everywhere the Pontiff took time to greet, touch and speak to those who had gathered to see him and to hear him speak. In Montreal, the topics he spoke on were as varied as his audiences: he warned against drugs and premarital sex and encouraged his listeners toward courage, self-discipline and faith.

At St. Joseph's Oratory, Pope John Paul II urged the priests and seminarians gathered to help Canadians fight the "more selfish attitude to life" that has overtaken our society. He also prayed at the tomb of Brother André (*below*), who died in 1937 and was beatified two years ago.

The Pope honored Marguerite Bourgeoys, the founder of the Mother House of the Sisters of the Congregation and the first Canadian woman to be named a saint, with a visit to the Mother House. Later at Jarry Park, he declared Marie-Leonie Paradis, a nineteenth-century nun, blessed. Sister Marie-Leonie founded the Little Sisters of the Holy Family, a religious order dedicated to housekeeping for priests.

Jarry Park, former home of the Montreal Expos, was the site of the Pope's first mass in Montreal. Hundreds of thousands gathered under gray skies at the stadium.

In his homily at Jarry Park, the Pope, drawing on the example of Sister Marie-Leonie Paradis, called upon the laity to serve others.

At Notre-Dame Basilica (*opposite page*), the Holy Father received an emotional welcome from over 2,000 children, many of whom reached out to him as he passed.

This page: At Olympic Stadium, the Pope challenged those attending the youth rally to reject "artificial paradise—a whiff of smoke, a bout of drinking or drugs."

Opposite page: One of the children at Notre-Dame Basilica reached up to touch the Pontiff's face.

Previous pages: Hundreds of white-clad figures formed the triumphant symbol of a dove at a morality play performed before the Pope's speech at Olympic Stadium.

St. John's

John Paul II is the 264th occupant of the Chair of St. Peter, the Fisherman. In Flat Rock, Newfoundland, the Pope spoke compassionately and forcefully to modern-day fishermen, whose fleet he had come to bless. He called unemployment "an affront to the dignity of the individual for which no social assistance can fully compensate," and called for more cooperatives to give the fishermen "a voice in the decision-making affecting their own lives and the lives of their families."

Fishing has been a way of life for the largely Roman Catholic community of 950 people ever since the eighteenth century. Pope John Paul chose to visit the settlement because it is the site of the famous Grotto of Our Lady of Lourdes, built by the villagers who contributed their own labor to the project. The Pope prayed briefly at the shrine before blessing the fleet, which lay in a cross formation in the harbor. His words were carried to the boats by radio.

In Flat Rock, Newfoundland, the Pontiff prayed briefly before the Grotto of Our Lady of Lourdes (*opposite page*), and blessed the fishing boats in the harbour (*above*), before boarding the popemobile (*left*) and continuing his journey to St. John's.

The Pope celebrated mass at Quidi Vidi Lake before a crowd that was smaller than anticipated. It rained steadily through the service, and the Pope suggested that the crowd should give thanks for "this baptism." He praised the family and "those couples who generously endeavor to follow God's plan for human love as expressed in the Church's teaching."

Above: There were many emotional moments as the Pope met several thousand handicapped people at St. John's Memorial Stadium.
Opposite: At the Basilica of St. John the Baptist, the Pontiff spoke to almost 2,000 Newfoundland educators. "We cannot leave God at the schoolhouse door," he told them.

Pope John Paul's last stop in Newfoundland was a youth rally. It was a happy occasion, despite the rain which poured down on the performers (*above and left*). The Pope seemed pleased with the parka that was presented to him (*right*).

Moncton

At the Notre-Dame-de-l'Assomption Cathedral in Moncton on Thursday, September 13, Pope John Paul addressed a group of about 1,500, many of whom were descendants of the Acadians, the original Roman Catholic settlers in the area.

Many of the Acadians who were driven from their homes by the British in the eighteenth century returned to the area after the Treaty of Paris in 1763. The Pope compared them to other groups that have suffered for their faith and national ties: "Despite the trials of deportation and even the threat of annihilation because of political vicissitudes, the Acadians remained faithful to their faith, faithful to their culture, faithful to their land."

Later, in the open-air mass at Magnetic Hill, the Pope spoke passionately to 100,000 followers about life, death and tolerance. He said that Christians must not condone torture or violence. They must show respect for human rights, including the right to life from the moment of conception, the right to one's reputation, and freedom of conscience.

The magnificent altar at Magnetic Hill, which was built on an empty site by the city of Moncton, included twin staircases and a waterfall and will remain as a shrine to the Pope.

At Notre-Dame-de-l'Assomption Cathedral (*left, above and overleaf*), the Pontiff praised those who remain true to their faith, as had the ancestors of many of those present in the Acadian city of Moncton. Before the Pope spoke, four New Brunswick residents, a teacher, a policeman, a homemaker and a nun, told him about their province and their concerns.

The mass in New Brunswick was held in a specially constructed site near the famous Magnetic Hill, about eleven kilometers from Moncton. Before the altar (*above*) was a waterfall flanked by two curved staircases. In what was to become a recurring theme during the tour, the Pope spoke of the crisis of values our society faces and called for a revival of faith.

Halifax

Cold and rainy weather dogged the papal tour, but it did not dampen the spirits of Pope John Paul or those who came to see him in Halifax.

Upon his arrival in Nova Scotia's capital, the Pope attended a spirited youth rally of 70,000 at the huge Central Commons park. He spoke to the young people about showing consistency between their faith and conduct, and urged them to "forge the bonds of justice and peace." Later that night, in a meeting with hundreds of lay ministers at St. Mary's Basilica, he called for a rejection of abortion, unmarried sex and divorce, as well as materialism and consumerism.

In the morning Pope John Paul visited sick children and the handicapped at the Izaac Walton Killam Hospital where he toured the wards and stopped to talk to individual patients. He then celebrated the eucharist back at Central Commons, where he paid homage to Canada's Catholic missionaries around the world.

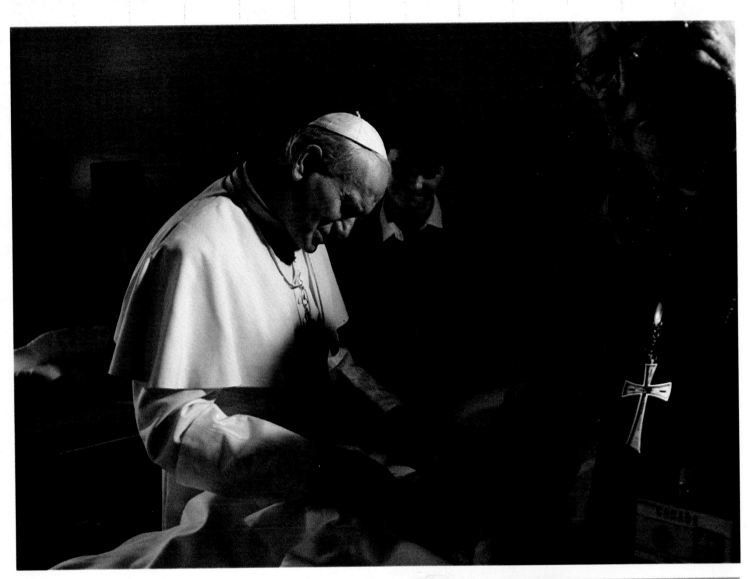

The Pope visits children at the
Izaac Walton Killam Hospital in
Halifax.

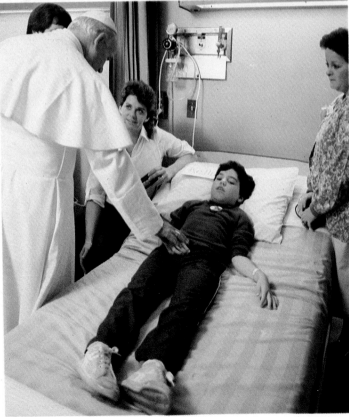

The open-air mass at Central
Commons.

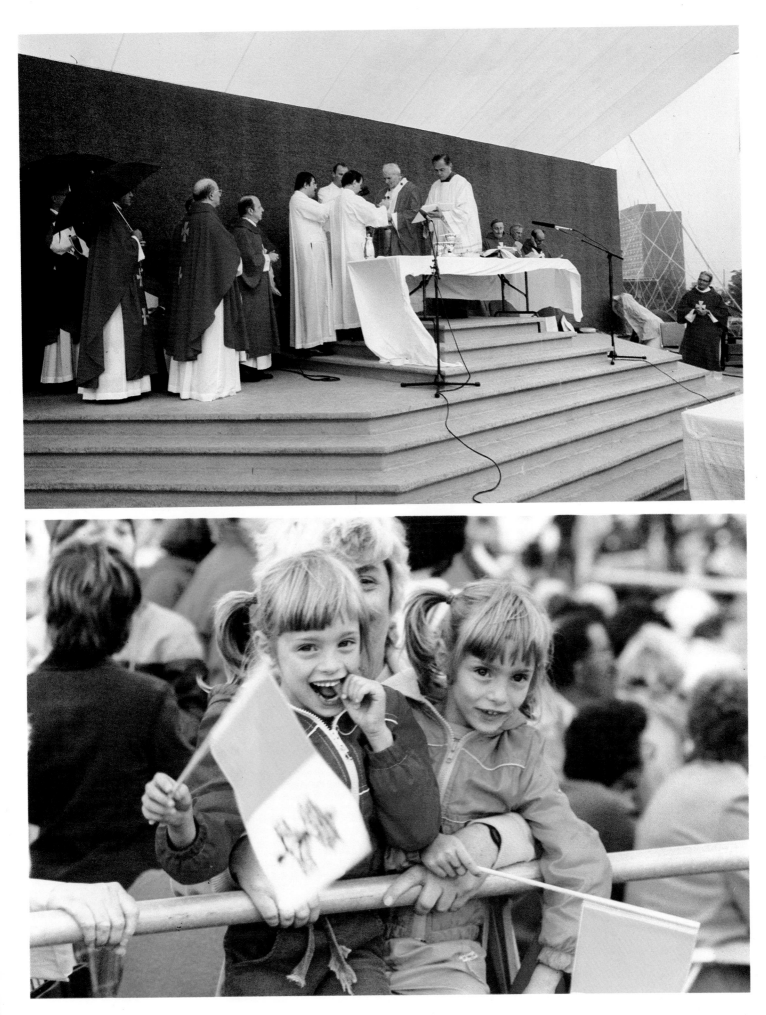

Toronto

In Toronto, which the Pontiff called the "heartland of Canada's industrial and technological development," the hectic pace continued, beginning with the lighting of a peace flame at City Hall. For two days the Pope traveled about the city and the surrounding area, meeting with clergy, political leaders, native groups and with the thousands who came to see him. The themes of his messages continued to relate to the moral and social order, and included the strength of faith, the importance of family and cultural identity, and human rights.

At Exhibition Stadium he spoke to 60,000 Canadians and Americans of Polish descent. Putting aside his prepared speech, he spoke passionately in support of Poland's outlawed trade union, Solidarity. All countries, he said, must work towards a universal declaration of human rights.

Earlier in the day he addressed more than 2,000 dignitaries of church and state at an ecumenical service in St. Paul's Anglican Church. The needs of the poor, he told them, must take priority over the desires of the rich.

The next day, he journeyed to Midland, where the missionaries Jean de Brébeuf and Gabriel Lalemant were martyred. Then he returned to Downsview, north of Toronto, for a mass before the largest crowd gathered together in Canadian history.

On his arrival in Toronto, Pope John Paul II was met by Gerald Emmett Cardinal Carter, Archbishop of Toronto, among other dignitaries, and traveled by popemobile (*left*) into the city.

79

At City Hall, the Pontiff lit a peace flame with fire brought from the Hiroshima Park in Japan.

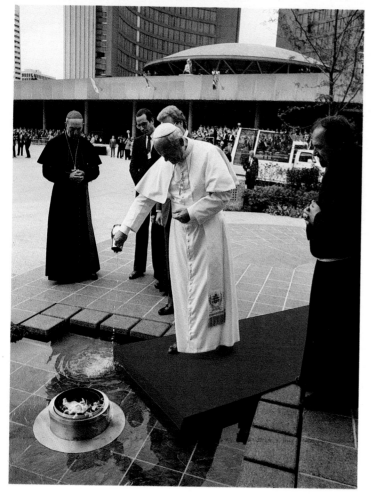

Previous pages: At St. Michael's Cathedral in Toronto, the Pope met with priests, cardinals and bishops, some from the United States. He stressed the importance of celibacy, which he called "a sign of freedom that exists for the sake of service." *Above:* Later, at St. Paul's Anglican Church, he spoke to an audience that included members of many denominations as well as many political leaders.

Speaking in his native Polish, the Pope (*opposite above*) addressed a large crowd of Polish Canadians and Americans at Exhibition Stadium on the evening of September 14. Those gathered watched the dancers (*overleaf*) and waved flags and banners (*right*). When the Pope noticed a banner with the word *Solidarnosc* he put aside his text and spoke of the importance of the word *solidarity* as a symbol and a reality.

Huronia, 160 kilometers north of Toronto, was once the center of the Great Lakes fur trade. In the seventeenth century, the Jesuits opened missions among the Hurons. During the bloody warfare between the Hurons and the Iroquois, a number of priests were martyred. At Midland, Pope John Paul II visited the reconstructed longhouse (*opposite*), the Martyr's Shrine (*right*) and the graves of Jean de Brébeuf and Gabriel Lalemant (*below*).

At a ceremony at the Midland shrine, the Pope spoke of a reconciliation between the Church and the Indians and praised Indian values and culture. An Iroquois elder presented him with an eagle feather, the symbol of the Great Spirit.

An estimated half million people were on hand at Downsview to welcome the Pope when he arrived by helicopter from Midland. Some had waited all night.

Standing under a twenty-four-meter-high white steel cross at Downsview, Pope John Paul challenged leaders in all fields to ensure that technology serves rather than enslaves humanity.

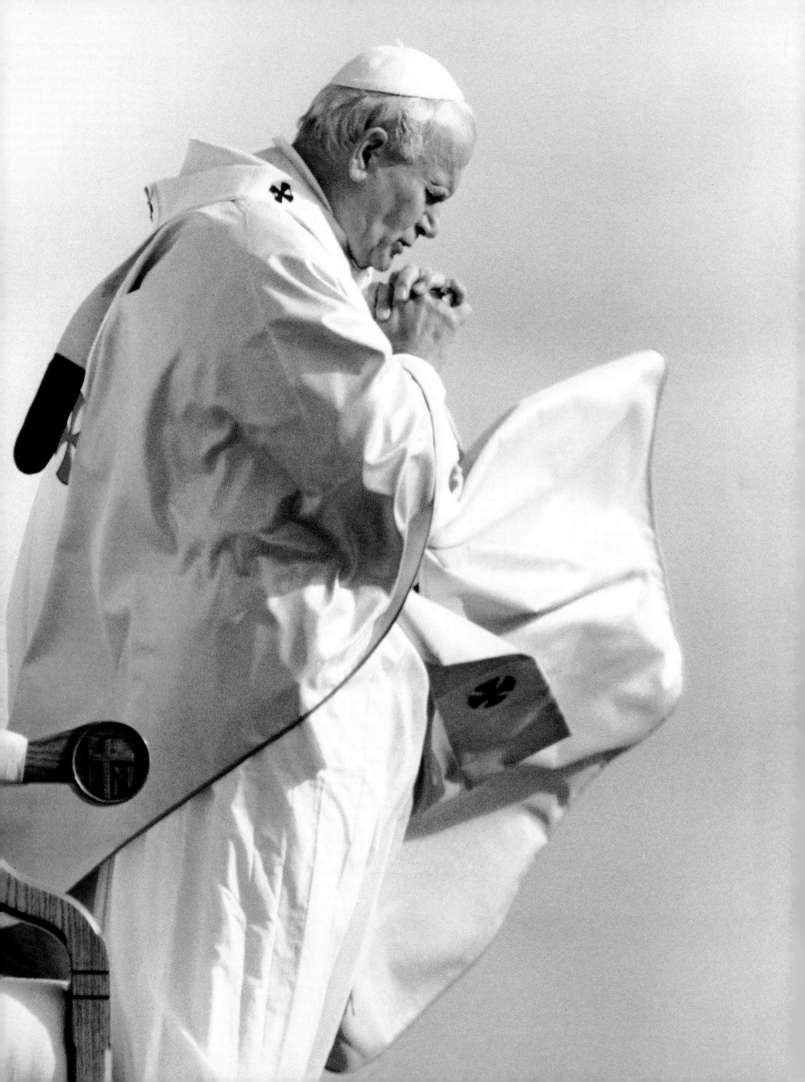

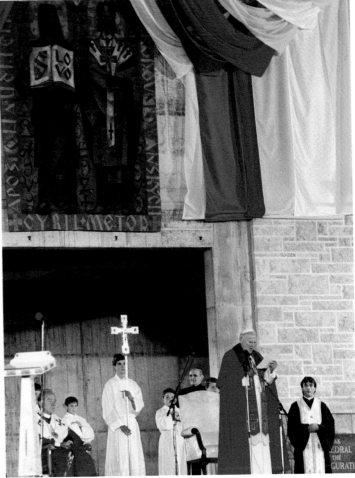

In the evening after the Downsview mass, the Pope visited the Cathedral of the Transfiguration of Our Lord, the church of Toronto's Slovak Byzantine Catholics. The Pope came to bless the church, which was still under construction.

A group of children (*above*) presented flowers and greetings to the Pope at the beginning of the ceremony at the Byzantine Church. During the consecration of the new cathedral, the Pope blessed the Antimension (*opposite above*), which corresponds to the altar stone in the Latin rite churches. It is made of fine linen or silk and is decorated with pictures of the burial of Christ and the instruments of His Passion.

Later that evening, the Pope visited Toronto's new convention center (*right*), where he was presented with many gifts, including an amethyst mounted in marble. Ontario Premier William Davis addressed the assembled dignitaries.

Winnipeg

Early in the morning of Sunday, September 16, Pope John Paul II left Toronto for Winnipeg, the Manitoba capital. The first stop of his day-long stay in the city was the Saints Vladimir and Olga Cathedral where he met with 1,200 Ukrainian Catholics. Speaking in Ukrainian, he praised Ukrainian pioneers, who "brought with them to Canada their strong Catholic faith," and urged his listeners to preserve their heritage of culture and faith. Afterwards, he went to St. Mary's Cathedral for the noon prayer. There he was presented with the St. Boniface General Hospital research foundation award for his efforts to encourage humanitarian uses of technology, science and medicine. The award was given him by a Catholic nun, a Jewish businessman and a Presbyterian lawyer.

An open-air mass that afternoon at Birds Hill Provincial Park was attended by 200,000 people who heard the Pope call for recognition of language rights, a contentious issue in the province.

Calling himself "a brother Slav," Pope John Paul II greeted Canada's seven Ukrainian bishops and a large gathering at Saints Vladimir and Olga Cathedral. He spoke to them in Ukrainian, praising their religious traditions and cultural heritage.

At an open-air mass before 150,000 in Winnipeg, the Pope spoke in French and English and offered hope for the "moral unity of this society." Once again he praised Canada's cultural diversity.

Edmonton

In Edmonton, the Pope was greeted by religious and political leaders from Alberta and Saskatchewan. Then he hurried on to an inter-faith service at St. Joseph's Basilica where members of many faiths—Christian, Jewish and Muslim among them—awaited him. Along the route were a number of stages where ethnic dancers performed. At the service the Pope spoke eloquently about all religions and especially about the "new and lasting covenant" between God and man. The first duty of all creatures, he said, is to glorify the Creator.

At an open-air mass attended by 140,000 the Pontiff delivered an angry speech urging a deeper commitment to worldwide sharing of wealth, especially between the nations of the North and those of the South.

The Pope had a scheduled afternoon of rest while in Edmonton. It was speculated that he would travel to the Rocky Mountains for fishing or hiking, both pastimes the Pontiff enjoys. Instead, he spent some time walking in Elks Island Provincial Park near Edmonton.

Previous pages: At an interfaith service Sunday night at St. Joseph's Basilica, the Pope was greeted by thunderous applause. At the service were 1,100 members of the clergy, whom the Pope greeted as brothers and sisters.

These pages: At the open-air mass in Edmonton, the Pontiff warned of the increasing disparity between rich and poor in the world and made a plea for peace and justice for all.

The Alberta mass, held in Namao, in what had been a farmer's field, attracted more than 140,000. Some arrived before sunrise in order to be near the impressive three-tier, seven-meter-high, blue and white altar. Above it was a canopy shaped like a dove in flight. After Edmonton, the Pope's next stop was to have been Fort Simpson, but fog prevented the plane from landing.

Vancouver

On his way to Vancouver, Pope John Paul II was scheduled to stop at Fort Simpson in the Northwest Territories. The plane circled but was unable to land in the heavy fog.

After an open-air mass at Abbotsford Airport near Vancouver in the afternoon, the Pope attended a rally, called a Celebration of Life, at B.C. Place. Taking up the theme, the Pope spoke of the region's abundance of natural life and of the rich cultural diversity of human life that characterizes the area. The emphasis of the evening was on the young, the elderly and the disabled, and the Pope had a special message for each group. The crowds cheered and roared their approval, and Pope John Paul in turn thanked them for their "outpouring of love."

On the return trip east to Ottawa, the Pontiff's plane again attempted unsuccessfully to land at Fort Simpson. Instead, it stopped to refuel in Yellowknife, where John Paul told those who had heard of his unexpected arrival and rushed to the airport that he had no special message for them, only a blessing. The speech he was to have given in Fort Simpson, which was broadcast instead over television, contained a message for the Dene and Inuit: all people, the Pope said, have a right to a land base and a share in the decision-making that affects them.

On his arrival in Vancouver, the Pope traveled by helicopter to Abbotsford, a municipal airport in the Fraser Valley, west of Vancouver, where a mass was to be celebrated. The crowd of over 200,000 cheered, then listened to the Pope's homily. "The heart of Jesus reveals the fullness of the Divinity and calls man to share in it," he told them.

At Vancouver's domed stadium, B.C. Place, Pope John Paul was welcomed by an adoring crowd as he circled the stadium in a white truck (*above*). The 64,000 present were also treated to more than 2,000 entertainers, including ethnic dancers and the Vancouver Symphony Orchestra (*left*). An elder of the Salish Indian nation presented the Pope with a Talking Stick (*right*), which confers on its owner the authority to speak on public occasions.

The city of Yellowknife was surprised by the news that the papal plane was landing at its airport. A member of the Native Council of Canada managed to find a gift for the Pope—his own buckskin jacket—which the Pope promptly put on (*above*). Later he broadcast the speech he had intended to give in Fort Simpson (*right*).

Ottawa

At the nation's capital, the Pope was met by Brian Mulroney, the new Canadian Prime Minister, sworn in only three days before, and by Archbishop Joseph Plourde and a host of dignitaries. From the airport he went by limousine to a special barge that took him on a fifty-minute cruise down the Rideau Canal, past thousands of onlookers.

Later in Hull, Quebec, across the river from Ottawa, the Pontiff said mass for the nuns of the Convent of the Sisters of Jesus and Mary, a cloistered and contemplative order.

The Pope was not scheduled to speak at a reception at Rideau Hall that evening, but he took the opportunity to urge the guests—senators, judges, members of Parliament and diplomats—to take advantage of their positions to promote a new vision of humanity and a new vision of peace. "One person cannot change the world," he told them, "but all of us together . . . will be able to create a peaceful and peace-loving society."

On the final day of the tour of Canada, the Pontiff met with Catholic bishops in the morning and celebrated mass at Lebreton Flats in the afternoon. As he left the country, he expressed his hope that his visit had inspired Canadians to a renewed humanity through God and to fraternal solidarity.

On his arrival in Ottawa, the Pontiff received a warm welcome from children (*previous pages*) and from a group of priests invited to the airport (*above*). As had happened many times on the trip, the Pope was soon surrounded by the children (*left*). From the airport, the Pope traveled to Dow's Lake, where he boarded a barge (*opposite above*) that took him past thousands gathered on the banks of the Rideau Canal (*right*).

This page: The Pope waved to crowds along the Rideau Canal. *Right:* At an evening reception given by the Governor General at Government House, the Pope spoke on the need for all men to unite for peace. Those in power, he said, must not close their eyes to the suffering of others.

At the Convent of the Sisters of Jesus and Mary (*this page and opposite above*), the Pope said mass for the nuns and told them that nuns should commit themselves to the "fruitfulness" of a life of service and obedience. The next day, the Pope met with Canada's bishops (*right*).

Pope John Paul II held his final mass in Canada at Lebreton Flats in Ottawa. He prayed for justice and peace and spoke movingly about the need for a "moral conscience" and a stop to the arms race.

Photo Credits

Arturo Mari, L'Osservatore Romano © Duomo Inc.:
pages 2, 5, 6, 8, 10-11, 12, 14 bottom, 20 top, 22-23, 25 top and bottom right, 26, 27, 30 top and bottom, 42 top, bottom left and bottom right, 45 bottom, 46-47, 49 top left and top right, 49 middle and bottom, 50, 52, 53 top and bottom, 54-55, 54 bottom left, 55, 56 top and bottom, 57, 58 bottom, 62, 63 top, 65, 67 top, 72, 73 bottom, 74 top, 75 top, 76, 78 top, 79 bottom, 80 top right, 81, 82, 84 top, 85 top and bottom, 86-87, 88 top and bottom, 89 top left, bottom left, bottom right, 91 bottom left, 101, 103 bottom, 105 top and bottom, 106, 109, 110-111, 112 top right, 113 top, 116, 117, 120 top and bottom, 124 top and bottom, 125 bottom, 126 top and bottom, 127, 131 top and bottom, 132, 134-135, 136 top and bottom, 137 bottom, 140 top and bottom left, 141 top and bottom, 142, 143 top

Pontificia Fotografic Felici © Duomo Inc.
pages 1, 15 top, 28 top and bottom, 29 top, 36-37, 43 top and bottom, 44 bottom left and bottom right, 54 bottom right, 58 top, 59, 64, 66-67, 73 top, 78 bottom, 79 top, 80 top left and bottom, 83 top and bottom, 89 top right, 91 top right and bottom right, 108 top left, middle left and bottom, 112 top left, 125 top, 128-129, 130, 137 top, 138 top, 139, 140 bottom right, 144 left

Boris Spremo, The Toronto Star:
pages 13 top and bottom, 14 top, 19 top, 24 top left, top right, and bottom right, 31, 32 top and bottom, 33 top and bottom, 34, 39 top and bottom, 60, 63 bottom, 67 bottom, 68-69, 96, 97 top, 114, 118 top and bottom left, 119 top and bottom, 122, 143 bottom, 144 right

David Cooper, The Toronto Star:
pages 15 bottom, 16-17, 18-19, 19 middle and bottom, 20 bottom, 21, 24 bottom left, 25 bottom left, 29 left middle, bottom left and right, 40, 70, 74 bottom, 75 bottom, 102-103, 103 top

Ron Bull, The Toronto Star:
pages 90, 91 top left, 108 top right and middle right, 112 bottom left and bottom right, 113 bottom, 118 bottom right, 121

Dick Loek, The Toronto Star:
pages 92 top and bottom left, 100

John Mahler, The Toronto Star:
pages 84 bottom, 94-95

Colin McConnell, The Toronto Star:
pages 92 bottom right, 93

Reg Innell, The Toronto Star:
page 138 bottom

Bob Olsen, The Toronto Star:
page 97 bottom

Mike Slaughter, The Toronto Star:
pages 98-99

Canapress Photo Service:
pages 38 top and bottom, 44 top and bottom middle, 45 top, and 48

Cavouk:
page 104

Governor General Jeanne Sauvé and Prime Minister Brian Mulroney and his wife Mila said goodbye to Pope John Paul II.